TSUNAMI
SURVIVAL STORIES

BY JEANNE MARIE FORD

childsworld.com

ABOUT THE AUTHOR

Jeanne Marie Ford is an Emmy-winning TV scriptwriter who holds an MFA degree in writing for children from Vermont College. She has written numerous children's books and articles, and she also teaches college English. She lives in Maryland with her husband and two children.

The Child's World
childsworld.com

Published by The Child's World®
800-599-READ • www.childsworld.com

Photography Credits
Photographs ©: Takeyuki Hitokoto/The Yomiuri Shimbun/AP Images, cover, 1; Gemunu Amarasinghe/AP Images, 5; Pacific Tsunami Museum/USGS, 6; Red Line Editorial, 8, 13, 20, 28 (Antarctica), 28–29; C. Storz/iStockphoto, 9; iStockphoto, 10, 23; Deddeda Stemler/CP/AP Images, 12; Walter Mooney/USGS, 14, 16; Shutterstock Images, 15, 25; Kyodo/AP Images, 18; Mass Communication Specialist 3rd Class Dylan McCord/US Navy, 22; Kurniawan Rizqi/Shutterstock Images, 24; Tatan Syuflana/AP Images, 26

ISBN Information
9781503854550 (Reinforced Library Binding)
9781503854802 (Portable Document Format)
9781503855182 (Online Multi-user eBook)
9781503855564 (Electronic Publication)

LCCN 2023937092

Printed in the United States of America

BRINGING THE WORLD TO YOUNG READERS 1968

CONTENTS

WHAT IS A TSUNAMI?

A tsunami is a series of long waves caused by the **displacement** of the ocean by a sudden force, such as an earthquake. Tsunamis can also be caused by volcanoes, landslides, and severe weather. Tsunami waves move from the bottom of the ocean up to its surface, traveling in multiple directions. They can cross entire oceans. Most are less than 10 feet (3 m) tall, but some are up to 100 feet (30.5 m) tall.

A tsunami approaching land may look more like a wall of water than a wave. The first wave may be followed by more waves. Tsunamis are dangerous when they rush onto land and **recede** into the sea. They can sweep people away and leave floating **debris** such as cars and trees. This debris can injure people caught in the floodwater. Flooding from a tsunami can extend more than 1 mile (1.6 km) from shore.

Warning signs before a tsunami include earthquakes, a roar coming from the ocean, and unusual changes in sea levels. When a tsunami danger is present, people should **evacuate** to higher ground and get far away from the water.

FAST FACTS

- On May 23, 1960, a tsunami caused by an earthquake in Chile struck Hilo, Hawaii. Sixty-one people were killed.
- On December 26, 2004, an earthquake off the coast of Sumatra, Indonesia, created a tsunami that barreled across the Indian Ocean. About 225,000 people in 12 countries died.
- On February 27, 2010, an earthquake struck off the coast of Chile. The resulting tsunami killed more than 500 people.
- On March 11, 2011, an earthquake off the coast of Honshu, Japan, caused a tsunami that left around 19,300 people dead.
- On December 22, 2018, the volcano Anak Krakatau erupted and partially collapsed, causing a tsunami. It hit the Sunda Strait region of Indonesia, killing about 437 people.

CHAPTER ONE

TWO MIRACLES

On May 22, 1960, a huge earthquake struck southern Chile. Fusayo Ito lived thousands of miles away in Hilo, a coastal city on the Big Island of Hawaii. The earthquake sent large waves across the Pacific Ocean, creating a tsunami. That night, a tsunami warning reached Hawaii. Sirens rang out in Hilo.

◄ **The 1960 tsunami caused about $75 million of damage in Hawaii's Hilo Bay area. It destroyed hundreds of businesses and homes.**

The Big Island had seen a fair number of tsunamis in the past. Ito's home was in an area far enough from shore that it was considered safe from tsunamis. But Ito was worried about some of her friends. She invited several of them to her house to stay with her until the danger had passed. They listened to news on the radio and chatted for hours.

By 1:00 a.m., Ito's friends decided it must be safe to go back home. But just a few minutes after they left, Ito heard a loud roaring sound. A 35-foot (11 m) tall tsunami was at her door. It smashed into her house. As the house fell down around Ito, something hit her head. She lost **consciousness**. When Ito woke up, she was holding on to her screen door and floating in the Wailoa River.

Ito was terrified. She didn't know how to swim. She held on to the screen door tightly as she rode up and down the choppy waves in darkness, choking on sea water. The current pulled her along the river until it finally dumped her into nearby Hilo Bay.

When the sun came up, Ito saw that she had floated out past the **breakwater**, far from shore. She was surrounded by debris. But in the daylight, Ito felt a sudden sense of peace. Whatever happened, she would face it with calm and resolve.

A pilot spotted Ito and alerted the US Coast Guard. When Ito saw their boat approaching, she thought it must be a ghost ship. Only when she heard voices did Ito realize she was being rescued. She had been sure she would never see another person again. Later, at the hospital, Ito hugged everyone she met.

When Ito left the hospital, she moved in with her grown-up daughter. She was glad her daughter lived far from the ocean. Ito had lost everything she owned in the tsunami. While she was grateful to be alive, she was sad that she'd lost her savings bonds.

TRACKING THE 1960 TSUNAMI

The earthquake that struck Chile in 1960 was the strongest earthquake that had ever been recorded. It created tsunami waves that reached Hawaii 15 hours later and Japan 22 hours later.

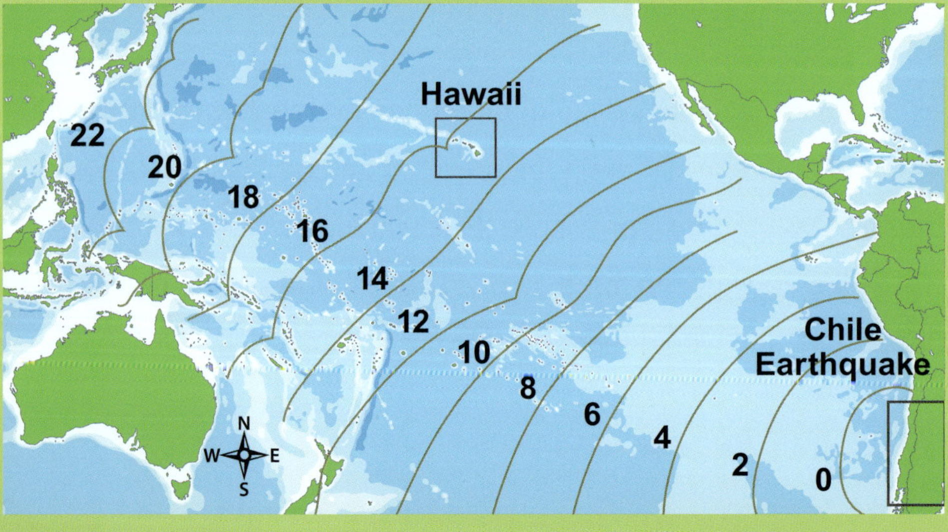

▲ **The Hilo Bay breakwater was built to help calm the water for ships in the bay. But the breakwater doesn't protect the city of Hilo from tsunamis.**

All of the money Ito had saved for her daughter's future was gone. But six months later, a worker found the savings bonds in a zippered satchel and returned them to Ito.

Ito thought it was a miracle that she was alive. Getting her savings bonds back was a second miracle. She was filled with gratitude and vowed to spend the rest of her life helping others. Ito volunteered for many organizations. In her late nineties, she was still volunteering weekly at the Pacific Tsunami Museum. She is remembered there for her positive attitude and kind smile.

CHAPTER TWO

NEVER BEFORE OR AGAIN

On the morning of December 26, 2004, Wittaya Tantawanich was working his shift on a rescue truck near Patong Hospital in Patong, Thailand. He decided to get some breakfast near the beach. As he was enjoying the ocean view, he felt an earthquake.

◀ **Phuket, Thailand, is home to many popular seaside resorts and beaches, including Patong Beach. The 2004 tsunami struck this area with little warning, killing 2,000 tourists.**

But the shaking wasn't strong enough to worry Tantawanich or anyone around him.

Two hours later, Tantawanich heard some nearby food vendors talking about catching fish. Then he saw that the shoreline had receded far into the ocean. Fish flopped around on the sand. At first, he laughed at the strange sight. But soon, Tantawanich realized something was very wrong. Suddenly, the water started rushing back onto the beach. It kept coming, far past where the shoreline had been. A vendor yelled at everyone to run as far and as fast as they could.

This tsunami didn't look like the giant waves Tantawanich had seen in pictures or on TV. It seemed more like a flash flood, pushing huge amounts of water onto the shore. The water started spreading faster as it reached the street.

Tantawanich jumped into his truck and sped uphill. On his walkie-talkie, someone informed him that another wave had struck. Tantawanich didn't know what was happening or why. But he knew he needed to head back toward the beach to help people.

Tantawanich was soon called to a supermarket near the beach. The market's basement had flooded. Some workers were trapped inside the basement. Many of them had already drowned.

▲ **The tsunami caused flooding in resort buildings along Patong Beach, filling up hotel lobbies and rooms with water. Many people were trapped or drowned.**

As Tantawanich worked to help people who were trapped and injured, he heard the rumble of another approaching wave. He stood still and prayed, sure that he was about to die. But the wave stopped at the street. He was safe.

Later, Tantawanich reflected that he had seen many scary and dangerous situations while on the job as a rescue worker. But he had never seen anything like the great Indian Ocean tsunami. He hoped he never would again.

INDIAN OCEAN TSUNAMI VICTIMS

The Indian Ocean tsunami affected people in many countries across the Indian Ocean. Most of those who died or were missing were from Indonesia.

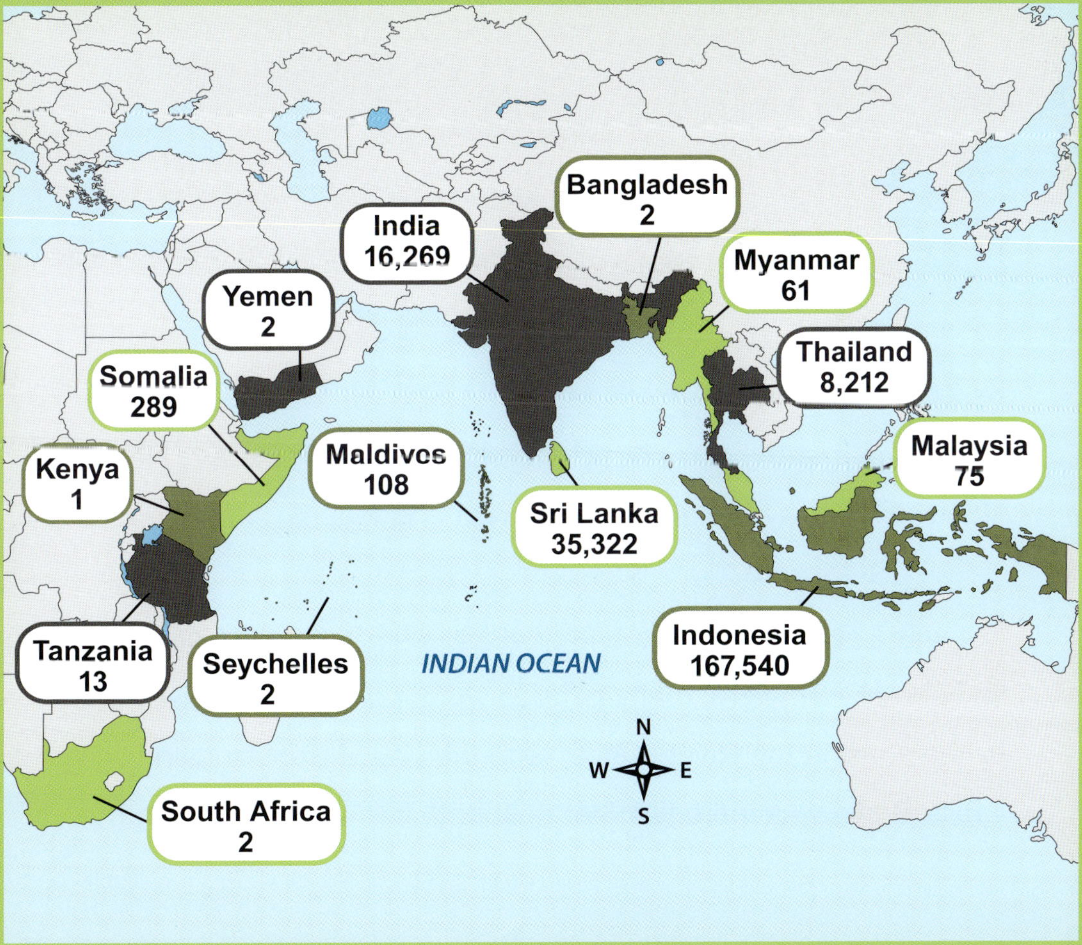

CHAPTER THREE

A HEROIC SACRIFICE

It was late February, the end of summer in Chile. On Saturday, February 27, 2010, many families were camping on an island by the coast in the River Maule, near the city of Constitución. Tabita Bravo was there with her husband, her son, and a friend.

◀ **Many boats along Chile's coast were carried inland by the 2010 tsunami. Some boats ended up on streets.**

They were sound asleep before being shaken awake by a powerful earthquake at 3:30 a.m.

Bravo's husband, Pedro Muñoz, had been a fisherman his whole life. As he saw the water being sucked away from the shore, he knew immediately that a tsunami was coming. He also knew that he and his companions weren't safe on the beach. They needed to get off the island before the wave hit.

HOW TSUNAMI WAVES TRAVEL

In the deep ocean, tsunami waves travel very quickly. A tsunami's speed slows in shallower water as it approaches land. The lengths of its waves decrease, while its wave heights increase.

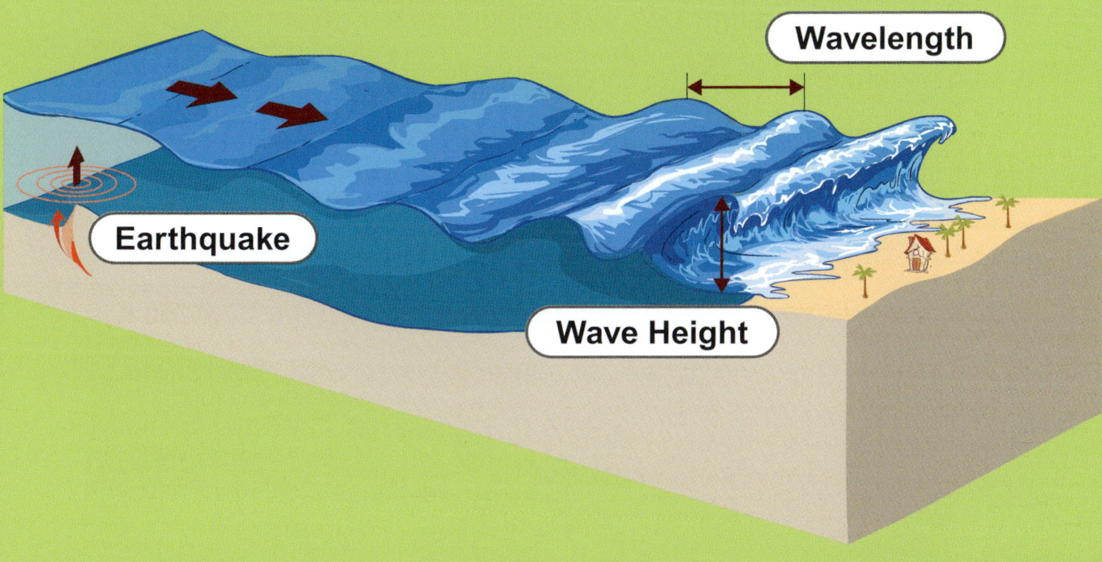

▲ **The tsunami damaged more than 400,000 homes along the coast of Chile, especially in the Maule and Biobío regions.**

Muñoz and Bravo's son, Luis, dragged their boat to the water's edge. They yelled for women and children to get into the boat first. Bravo ran to gather people camping nearby. But there wasn't enough room in the boat for everyone.

Bravo helped four women and six children onto the boat as a large wave approached. She watched as Muñoz **navigated** over the wave and got his passengers safely to the mainland's shore, which was 200 yards (180 m) away. Muñoz guided the boat back to the island. This time, Bravo climbed on board with nine others.

Luis and the family's friend stayed to continue gathering people for the next trip.

A second wave rolled in as Muñoz's boat reached the mainland again. Bravo heard people screaming. She shouted to Luis, telling him to climb a tree. He shouted back that he was OK and that he loved her.

Bravo begged her husband not to go back to the island. He had already saved 20 people. But a neighbor pleaded with Muñoz to make one more trip to rescue people who were still stranded. Muñoz told his wife that he couldn't live with himself if he didn't try to save them.

Bravo watched Muñoz leave once again and waited near a bridge for him to return. Then she heard a third wave coming. She heard the snapping sound of boats tearing loose from their docks. Terrified, she ran uphill. When she looked back, she saw that Muñoz and his boat weren't there. Luis and the friend had been swept away, too. In that moment, Bravo knew they were gone forever.

Muñoz's body was found six days later. Bravo lost her husband and son. Most of her possessions were destroyed by the tsunami, too. She held tight to three family photos that she pulled from the muddy remains of her home. She would always remember her husband as a hero.

CHAPTER FOUR

RAINBOW AFTER THE STORM

Shiori Takeyama was a fourth grader at Okawa Elementary School in Ishinomaki, Japan. The students in her class were all turning ten that year. They celebrated their Half Coming-of-Age Ceremony with their parents in early March. The students looked forward to marking their full Coming-of-Age when they turned 20.

At the school ceremony, they read letters of thanks to their mothers. They ran out of time to sing a song they'd practiced called "Arigato," which means "Thank You." Their teacher decided to record the song and give it to the students' parents on a CD.

On March 11, 2011, the class was making the CD recording after school. The children were about to start singing the song's second verse when the ground started shaking. The power went out in the building. The students screamed and scurried under their desks to take cover. Finally, the earthquake was over.

◀ **The 2011 Japan tsunami devastated Okawa Elementary School, tearing off walls, toppling columns, and leaving debris on the roof.**

2011 TSUNAMI WAVE HEIGHTS

The wave heights of a tsunami depend on how far away the waves are from the site of the earthquake. During the 2011 Japan tsunami, regions closer to the earthquake experienced taller and more destructive waves.

The students followed the teacher's directions to evacuate the building. They were still wearing their indoor slippers.

Shiori and her classmates hurried down the stairs and ran outside to the playground. Some were crying as the teacher started taking roll call. Shiori worried about her family. What if her house had fallen down in the earthquake? Or what if her mother had been hurt or killed?

Shiori was greatly relieved when her mother came to the school a few minutes later. She asked Shiori if she wanted to go home. Shiori felt scared, so she said yes. Most of her friends were still on the playground as she and her mother drove away.

Suddenly, Shiori saw water on the road. Her mother recognized the signs of a tsunami. She immediately turned her car around and headed for higher ground. The tsunami slammed into the school at 3:37 p.m. The clocks inside stopped at that time as they were flooded with water. Seventy-four of the school's 108 students died in the tsunami, along with ten staff members.

Shiori's whole life changed in that moment. Most of her friends were gone. She couldn't go back to school for more than a month, until Okawa Elementary rented space in another school for its remaining students. Shiori and her classmates spent one day every month remembering their friends who had died in the tsunami. They wrote letters, sang songs, and told stories.

Osaka

▲ **The ruins of Okawa Elementary School are still standing. The site is now a memorial for the students and teachers who lost their lives in the tsunami.**

In her school bag, Shiori always carried a photo of her class that had been taken under the cherry trees.

Shiori felt that her life was divided into two parts—before the tsunami and after it. She was comforted when she dreamed of playing with her friends. When she was old enough to drive, she would sometimes visit what was left of Okawa Elementary. Being there stirred happy memories. Shiori remembered riding unicycles around the playground with friends and eating cupcakes after playing musical chairs. One day when she was visiting, a rainbow appeared over the school. It made her feel happy and at peace.

◄ **After the tsunami, rescue teams, firefighters, and volunteers searched for survivors in the wreckage.**

CHAPTER FIVE

SWEPT AWAY

On the night of December 22, 2018, white strobe lights flashed outside a seaside resort in Java, an island in Indonesia. The moon was full. A warm breeze blew. Guests strolled past tables covered with white cloths as a band celebrated the year's end. The band's lead singer held a long note as the guitarist strummed.

◄ **The concert hit by the 2018 tsunami took place at the Tanjung Lesung beach resort in Java's Banten province. The force of the waves littered the beach with debris.**

A woman used her cell phone to take a video. Laughter floated from another area of the lawn, where a comedian was performing.

Suddenly, a giant wall of water rushed toward the partygoers. The wave tossed the band members and their instruments into the audience. It killed many of the resort guests in an instant.

The tsunami had been caused by the volcano Anak Krakatau, which was located about 20 miles (32 km) off the coast of Java.

HOW DID A VOLCANO CAUSE A TSUNAMI?

In early 2018, eruptions of the Anak Krakatau volcano caused lava to collect on its southern side. The weight of this lava led part of the volcano to collapse into the ocean. This collapse generated a powerful tsunami.

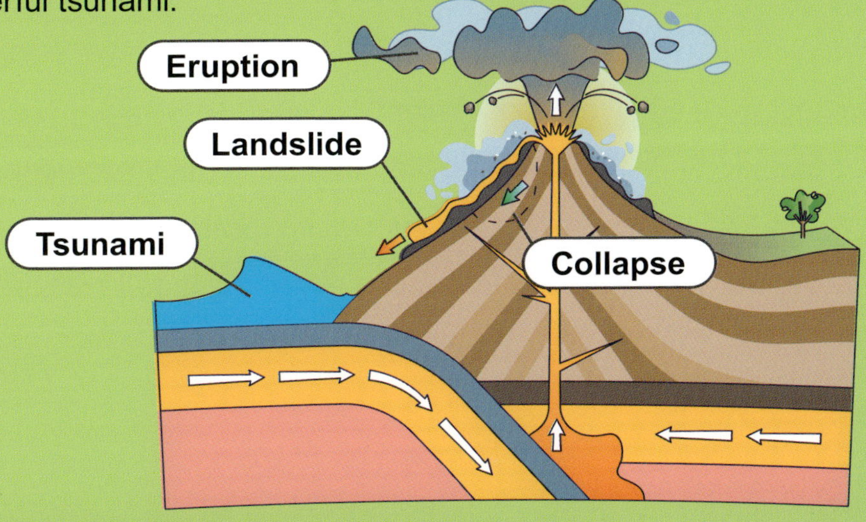

▲ **After the tsunami, volunteers, soldiers, and rescue teams searched the beaches for survivors and bodies.**

A piece of the volcano collapsed and displaced ocean water. Because there was no earthquake **preceding** the wave, it came without warning in the dark of night.

Mamad Setiadi had helped the band set up its equipment. When he saw water rolling toward him, he climbed a tree. From above, Setiadi watched in horror as seawater flooded the stage.

He saw the ocean overtake everything. It covered trees and cars. It drowned men, women, and children.

When the water rushed back into the ocean, Setiadi watched survivors struggle to hold on so they would not be swept up by the sea. When it was over, most of the band members were dead. So were the comedian and his wife. Left behind were twisted pieces of metal and broken speakers. Dirty white tablecloths were scattered around the lawn.

When he was sure it was safe, Setiadi climbed down from the tree. He raced home in terror, tripping over debris in the darkness. He would never forget the horrors he had seen that night.

THINK ABOUT IT

- What would you do if you found yourself in the path of a tsunami? Where would you go to stay safe? Why?
- How can you help people who have been impacted by tsunamis?
- Tsunamis can seriously injure or kill people. What do you think could be done to protect people from tsunamis?

TSUNAMI MAP

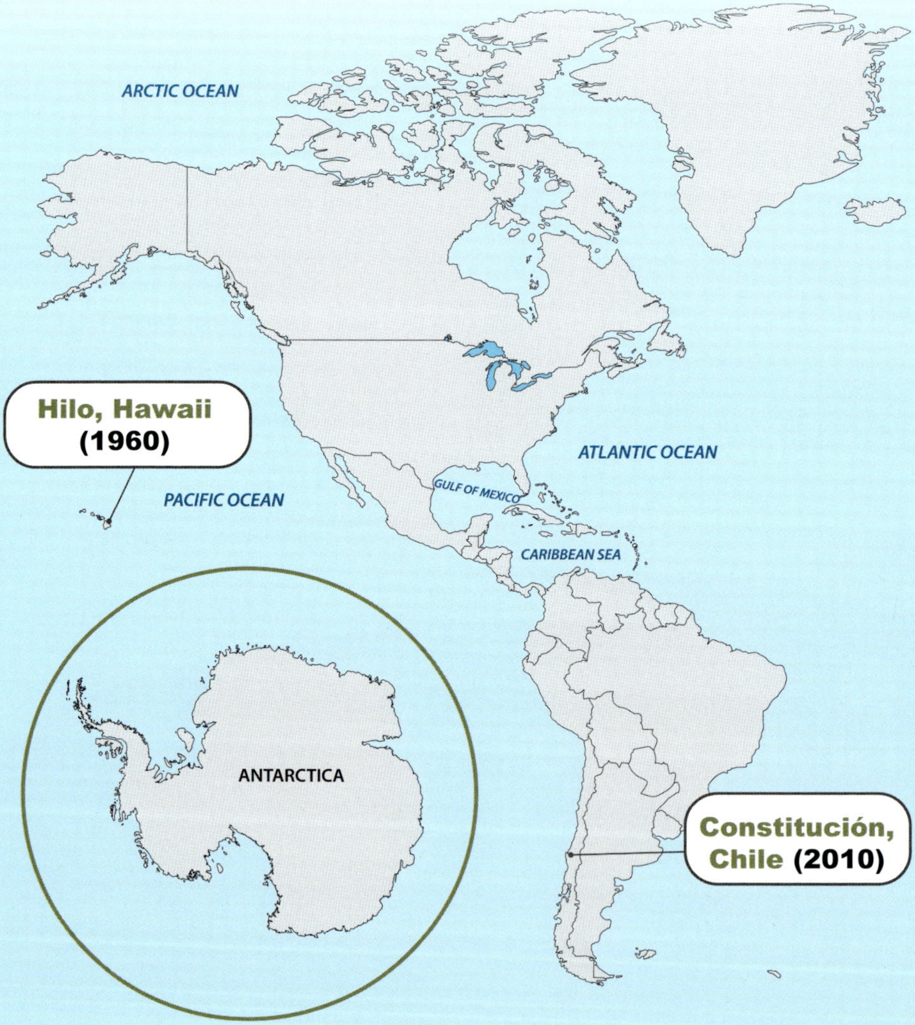
ARCTIC OCEAN
Hilo, Hawaii (1960)
PACIFIC OCEAN
ATLANTIC OCEAN
GULF OF MEXICO
CARIBBEAN SEA
ANTARCTICA
Constitución, Chile (2010)

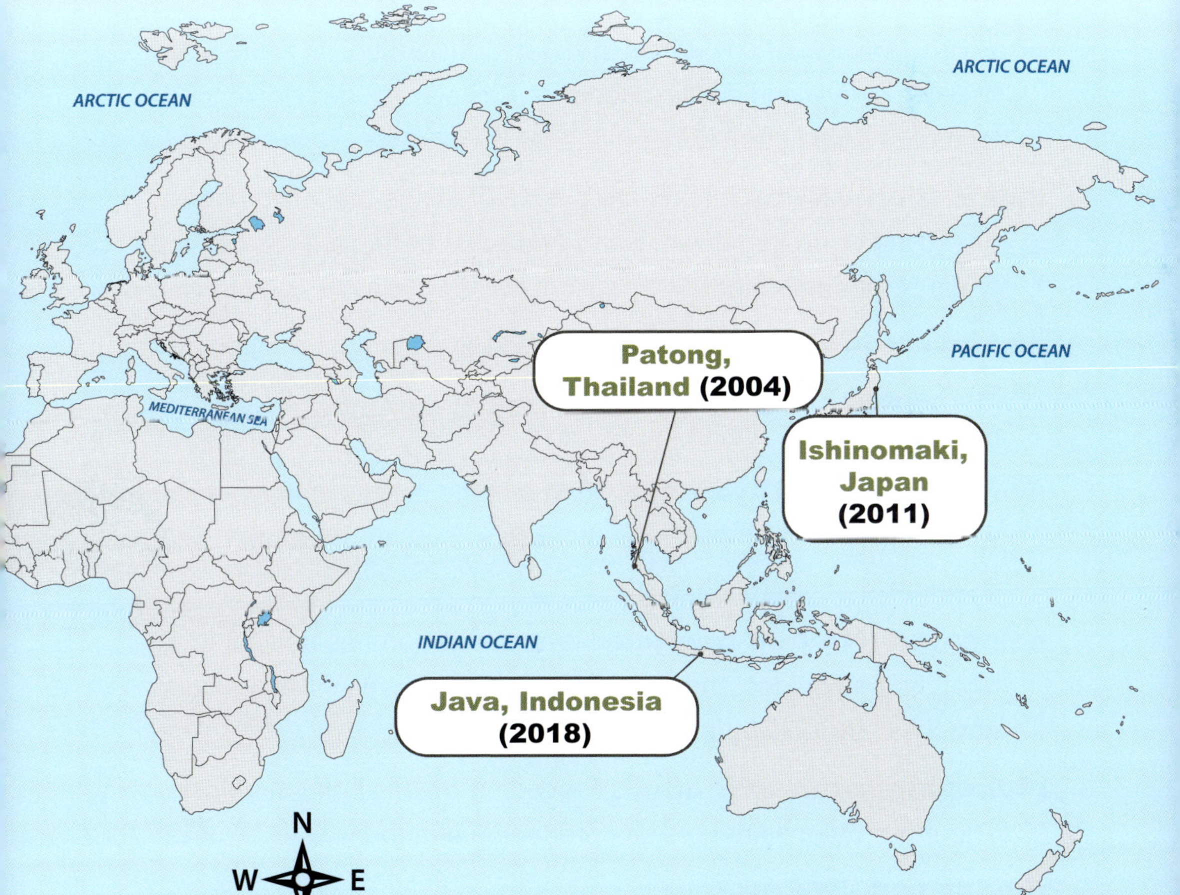
ARCTIC OCEAN
ARCTIC OCEAN
PACIFIC OCEAN
MEDITERRANEAN SEA
INDIAN OCEAN
Patong, Thailand (2004)
Ishinomaki, Japan (2011)
Java, Indonesia (2018)
N
W
E
S

GLOSSARY

breakwater (BRAYK-wah-ter): A breakwater is a barrier built to protect a beach from wave damage. The breakwater helped calm waves at the shore.

consciousness (KON-shus-ness): Consciousness is the state of being aware and awake. Head injuries can cause people to lose consciousness.

debris (duh-BREE): Debris are pieces of things that have been destroyed or broken down. Sand and parts of houses are common types of tsunami debris.

displacement (dis-PLAYSS-ment): Displacement happens when an object moves a liquid out of place. Water displacement in the ocean can cause a tsunami.

evacuate (eh-VAK-yoo-ayt): To evacuate means to leave a place where one might be in danger. If there is a tsunami warning, people should evacuate the area.

navigated (NAV-uh-gay-ted): When a person has navigated a boat, he has guided and steered it to its destination. Sailors once navigated by looking at the stars.

preceding (pruh-SEE-ding): Preceding means coming before. There are often warning signs preceding a tsunami.

recede (ruh-SEED): Recede means to go back from a position. After a tsunami hits, its waves recede into the ocean.

SELECTED BIBLIOGRAPHY

Sim, Vanessa. "Three Tsunamis That Changed Hilo and Hawaii's Big Island." *Hawai'i Magazine*, 25 Nov. 2009, hawaiimagazine.com. Accessed 4 Apr. 2023.

"Surviving a Tsunami—Lessons from Chile, Hawaii, and Japan." *USGS*, 2 July 2007, usgs.gov. Accessed 26 July 2023.

"Tsunamis." *National Oceanic and Atmospheric Administration*, 14 Apr. 2023, noaa.gov/education. Accessed 4 Apr. 2023.

FIND OUT MORE

BOOKS

Eason, Sarah. *Surviving the Tsunami: Hear My Story*. New York, NY: Crabtree, 2020.

Ford, Jeanne Marie. *Earthquake Survival Stories*. Parker, CO: The Child's World, 2024.

Squire, Ann O. *Tsunamis*. New York, NY: Scholastic, 2016.

WEBSITES

Visit our website for links about tsunamis:
childsworld.com/links

Note to Parents, Caregivers, Teachers, and Librarians: We routinely verify our Web links to make sure they are safe and active sites. So encourage your readers to check them out!

INDEX